SHOOT

THE VOICE OF FOOTBALL

ANNUAL EDITOR: David Clayton

f /TheVoiceOfFootball   WWW.SHOOT.CO.UK   🐦 @_shootfootball

CONTENTS

SHOOT FOR THE STARS

Before we move on, let's find out more about the real star of the Shoot Annual 2024 – you!

Fill in the page and keep it safe for future years so you can see how many of your dreams could come true!

THIS ANNUAL BELONGS TO...

3 TEAMS I'D LIKE TO PLAY FOR...

1.
2.
3.

3 TEAMS I'D LIKE TO PLAY AGAINST...

1.
2.
3.

3 PLAYERS I'D LIKE AS TEAMMATES...

1.
2.
3.

3 STADIUMS I'D LIKE TO PLAY AT...

1.
2.
3.

THE TROPHY I'D LOVE TO WIN IS...

MY DREAM MANAGER IS...

THE TEAM I PLAY FOR IS...

THE POSITION I PLAY IS...

YOUR RATINGS

Colour in the number of stars you think matches your skill levels!

SPEED	★★★★★
SHOOTING	★★★★★
PASSING	★★★★★
DRIBBLING	★★★★★
DEFENDING	★★★★★
TEAMWORK	★★★★★

LOUD & CROWD!

The 2023 Women's FA Cup final at Wembley Stadium between Chelsea and Manchester United attracted a record crowd of 77,390 – almost 32,000 more than the previous record set a year earlier.

KING KEV

Manchester City's Kevin De Bruyne became the fastest player in Premier League history to register 100 Premier League assists when his cross was headed home by Erling Haaland against Southampton in April 2023. He achieved the feat in just 237 games – 56 faster than the previous record holder, Cesc Fabregas.

FACTS,
& NUMBERS

Check out these memorable footy facts, stats and numbers from the biggest players and competitions this year!

ON MY HEAD!

Harry Kane set a new Premier League record for headed goals in one season when he nodded home his 10th of the season against Crystal Palace in May 2023. That goal also made him the Premier League's all-time second top scorer behind Alan Shearer.

SMASH AND GRAB!

When Nottingham Forest beat Arsenal in May 2023, they had just 18% possession, the lowest on record (since 2003–04) for a winning team in a Premier League match.

100 CLUB

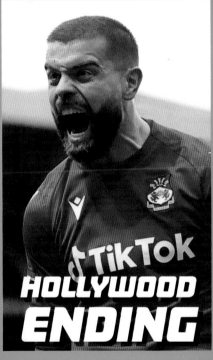

Vincent Kompany took Burnley back up to the Premier League after just one season outside the top division. In his debut season as boss at Turf Moor, the former Manchester City captain guided the Clarets to the Championship title in style, winning 29 of their 46 league games and amassing 101 points.

3 IS THE MAGIC NUMBER

Chelsea won their sixth league title on the final day of the season and became the first team to be crowned WSL champions three years in a row. Blues boss Emma Hayes has guided them to all three titles.

GREAT SCOT!

Celtic won their 53rd Scottish Premiership title in 2022/23, finishing well clear of Glasgow rivals Rangers. It was Celtic's 11th title in 12 years.

GOALS, GOALS GOALS!!!!!

The 2022–23 season was the highest-scoring 38-game season in Premier League history, with 1,084 goals (with a 2.85 goals per match ratio).

HOLLYWOOD ENDING

Wrexham won promotion to the Football League after 15 years of non-League football. Under the ownership of Hollywood stars Ryan Reynolds and Rob McElhenney, the Welsh side racked up 111 points to win the National League title. Notts County were also promoted, and their 107 points is a record amount for a runner up.

RECORD BREAKER!

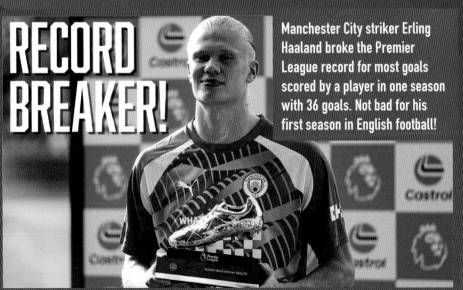

Manchester City striker Erling Haaland broke the Premier League record for most goals scored by a player in one season with 36 goals. Not bad for his first season in English football!

PENALTY SHOOT OUT

It's time to settle who has the best footy knowledge – you or your mate! In this penalty shoot-out there can only be one winner!

Get a 3rd person to act as the referee so they can tell you the correct answer after each penalty so you know the score as you go...

PENALTY 1

How many goals did Erling Haaland score on his Manchester City Premier League debut against West Ham United?

A: 1 goal
B: 2 goals
C: 3 goals

Your answer:
Your opponent:
Score after 1 penalty: ☐ – ☐

PENALTY 2

Liverpool thrashed Manchester United in the Premier League at Anfield in March 2023 – but by what score?

A: 6 - 0
B: 7 - 1
C: 7 - 0

Your answer:
Your opponent:
Score after 2 penalties: ☐ – ☐

PENALTY 3

How many managers did Leeds United have in the 2022/23 Premier League season?

A: 4 managers
B: 3 managers
C: 2 managers

Your answer:
Your opponent:
Score after 3 penalties: ☐ – ☐

PENALTY 4

Which Italian team knocked Spurs out of the Champions League in February 2023?

A: Inter Milan   B: Napoli   C: AC Milan

Your answer:
Your opponent:
Score after 4 penalties: ☐ – ☐

PENALTY 5

The fastest goal in the Premier League last season was scored after how many seconds?

A: 9 seconds   B: 15 seconds   C: 22 seconds

Your answer:
Your opponent:
Score after 5 penalties: ☐ – ☐

SUDDEN DEATH

If you are level after five penalties, here's a sudden death question –
What is the capacity of Wembley Stadium? The nearest to the actual capacity wins!

ANSWERS ON PAGES 76-77

FROM THE SPOT

How good is your memory of famous penalties? Can you figure out if the three players below scored or missed their crucial penalty kick by predicting what happened next! Can you remember where the ball ended up? Circle your answer.

PENALTY A

England v France
FIFA World Cup 2022, Quarter-final

Trailing 2-1 to France, England are in the ascendency and win a late penalty that, if converted, will almost certainly take the game into extra time. England captain Harry Kane has already scored from the spot on 54 minutes – can he do it again and hold his nerve?

MISS MISS MISS MISS MISS MISS MISS MISS

MISS MISS

TOP LEFT	TOP MIDDLE	TOP RIGHT
BOTTOM LEFT	BOTTOM MIDDLE	BOTTOM RIGHT

MISS MISS MISS

PENALTY B

England Women v Brazil,
UEFA Finalissima, Final, April 2023

European champions England take on South American champions Brazil at a packed Wembley Stadium and after Brazil grab a late equaliser, the game goes to penalties. Chloe Kelly has the chance to win the game. Can the Manchester City forward score the decisive penalty?

MISS MISS MISS MISS MISS MISS MISS MISS

MISS MISS MISS

TOP LEFT	TOP MIDDLE	TOP RIGHT
BOTTOM LEFT	BOTTOM MIDDLE	BOTTOM RIGHT

MISS MISS MISS

PENALTY C

Argentina v France
FIFA World Cup 2022, Final

Argentina have the chance to win the World Cup after France miss two of their penalty shoot-out spot-kicks and the score is 3-2 to Argentina. Can Gonzalo Montiel keep his nerve - or will France somehow stay alive?

MISS MISS MISS MISS MISS MISS MISS MISS

MISS MISS MISS

TOP LEFT	TOP MIDDLE	TOP RIGHT
BOTTOM LEFT	BOTTOM MIDDLE	BOTTOM RIGHT

MISS MISS MISS

ANSWERS ON PAGES 76-77

99

HAIRY STYLES

These six Premier League stars have decided to copy the hairstyle of one of their teammates – can you name the player and whose hairstyle they have copied?

A

Player:

Hairstyle:

B

Player:

Hairstyle:

C

Player:

Hairstyle:

D

Player:

Hairstyle:

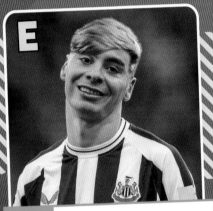

E

Player:

Hairstyle:

F

Player:

Hairstyle:

CELEBRATIONS

Who is behind these six famous celebrations?

A

Player:

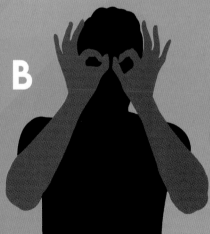

B

Player:

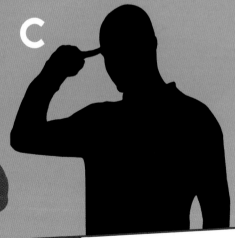

C

Player:

WHAT'S MY NUMBER?

Do you know the shirt numbers of the top players in the Premier League? It's not as easy as you might think! Choose the correct number for the correct player and write it on the back of the shirt.

ANSWERS ON PAGES 76-77

STERLING
26
DUNK
47
EZE

10
FODEN
17
ROBERTSON
ISAK

14
5

D

E

F

Player:

Player:

Player:

KIT KING

Here's your chance to design a new kit for the team you support or the team you play for. Don't hold back – go crazy with the design and colour to make your kit stand out from the rest!

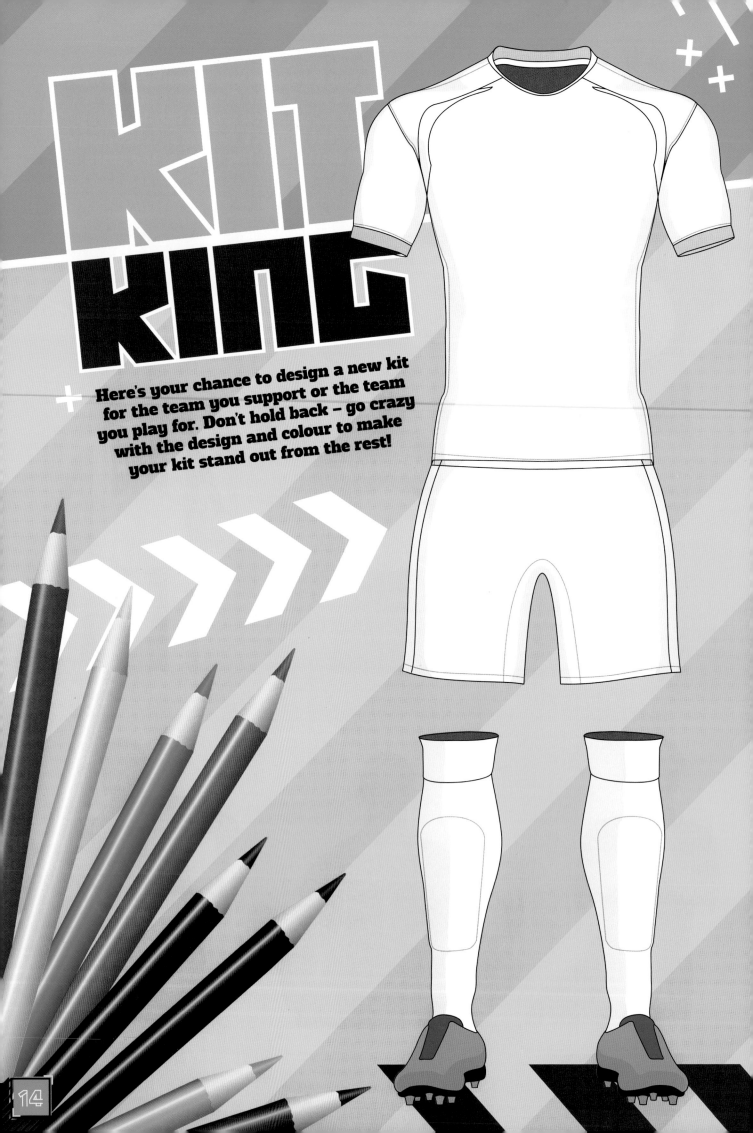

CAREER CHANGE

Most players play for many clubs in their career – so, can you name these four current stars just by looking at the teams they have played for? The further back you go in their careers, the harder it is to guess their identity!

1

QUEEN'S PARK > DUNDEE UNITED > HULL CITY > LIVERPOOL

THE PLAYER IS:
....

2

BIRMINGHAM CITY > BORUSSIA DORTMUND > REAL MADRID

THE PLAYER IS:
....

3

MANCHESTER UNITED > ARSENAL > WATFORD > BRIGHTON

THE PLAYER IS:
....

4

LIVERPOOL > MANCHESTER CITY > CHELSEA

THE PLAYER IS:
....

ANSWERS ON PAGES 76-77

15

CHAMPIONS LEAGUE

HIT OR MISS?

There's a glorious goalscoring chance in each of these Champions League pictures, but did the ball **HIT** the back of the net or was it a glaring **MISS**?

GAME 1: Rangers V Liverpool

HIT or MISS?

GAME 2: Manchester City V Real Madrid

HIT or MISS?

GAME 3: Chelsea V Real Madrid

HIT or MISS?

GAME 4: Arsenal V Wolfburg

HIT or MISS?

ANSWERS ON PAGES 76-77

CLUB: Newcastle United
COUNTRY: Brazil
POSITION: Central Midfield
BORN: 16 November 1997
PREVIOUS CLUBS: Audax, Athletico Paranaense, Lyon

DID YOU KNOW?

Guimaraes wears the number 39 shirt at Newcastle United because the taxi his father drove for more than 20 years in Rio di Janeiro was also number 39 – he wore the same number at Lyon as well!

BRUNO GUIMARAES

17

ERLING HAALAND

Erling Haaland scored 36 goals in 35 Premier League appearances –a new record for most goals in a single season which had previously been held by Andy Cole and Alan Shearer – and they reached their tally of 34 in a 42-game season.

English football has never seen anything quite like Manchester City's goal-scoring machine Erling Haaland – Shoot looks at some of his incredible achievements from his first season at the Etihad.

Erling managed back-to-back hat-tricks against Crystal Palace and Nottingham Forest and scored four in the Premier League in his first campaign, though Alan Shearer scored five for Blackburn in 1995-96 so that's a record he can break in 2023/24!

Erling scored more Premier League goals than Everton or Wolves managed in 38 games!

Erling won the Premier League Golden Boot in his first season with City, beating England skipper Harry Kane who bagged 30 for Spurs.

Erling is the first Premier League player to score hat-tricks in three successive home games – he managed the feat in the games against Crystal Palace, Nottingham Forest and Manchester United.

Erling has won the Champions League Golden Boot for 2022/23 with 12 goals – the second time he has won the award after managing it 2020/21 when he was aged only 20!

His 36 Premier League goals came from just 123 shots! A conversion rate of 29% and close to one goal from every three shots!

Erling scored an incredible FIVE goals in one Champions League game against Red Bull Leipzig – it took him just 35 minutes to achieve that tally and only Haaland and Lionel Messi have scored a first-half hat-trick in a Champions League knockout game.

Erling scored 52 goals in all competitions in 2022/23 – the most in one season by a Premier League player, ever! He smashed the previous record held by Mo Salah in 2017/18 and Ruud van Nistelrooy in 2002/03 who both scored 44.

Erling was voted the Premier League Player of the Season, the Premier League Young Player of the Season and won the Football Writers' Association Footballer of the Year award.

Swap back for a day!

These Premier League superstars had spells at smaller clubs – imagine if they could have them back just for one day. Well, thanks to Shoot, they can! With our rules, each club can have their superstar back for one game – and this is how it would look!

JACK GREALISH
NOTTS COUNTY

'Super Jack' became English football's first £100 million player when he joined Manchester City in 2022 – but in 2013/14, he played 39 games for Notts County during a season-long loan. City are loaning him back for 24 hours!

Record goal-scorer Harry Kane also knows the lower leagues well from his early years as a professional. In 2010/11, he spent six months on loan with League One side Leyton Orient, making 18 appearances and scoring five times. Now The O's can have Harry back for one game this season!

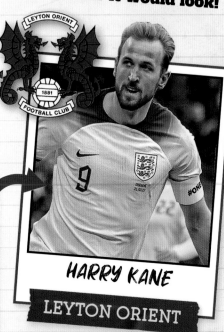

HARRY KANE
LEYTON ORIENT

Part of the Manchester City side that won the 2008 FA Youth Cup, Kieran Trippier had to have loan spells elsewhere to really make his name. In 2010, City loaned him to Barnsley where he made 44 appearances over the next year. The England full-back can take his set-piece specials back to Oakwell for one game this campaign!

KIERAN TRIPPIER
BARNSLEY

Martinez's progress from loan ranger to World Cup winner is a remarkable story. He joined the Gunners aged 18, but they sent the inexperienced teenager out on loan to learn his trade with Oxford, Sheffield Wednesday, Rotherham, Wolves and finally Reading in 2019. Having being relegated to League One, Reading fans would love to have a World Cup winner between the sticks, even just for one match!

JORDAN HENDERSON
COVENTRY CITY

Coventry City couldn't have imagined they had a future England captain on their books when they loaned Jordan Henderson from Sunderland in 2009. Henderson proved a popular player for the Sky Blues, playing 13 games and scoring his first senior goal. Would Henderson's leadership have helped Coventry in the Championship Play-Off Final if he came back for one game?

EMILIANO MARTINEZ
READING

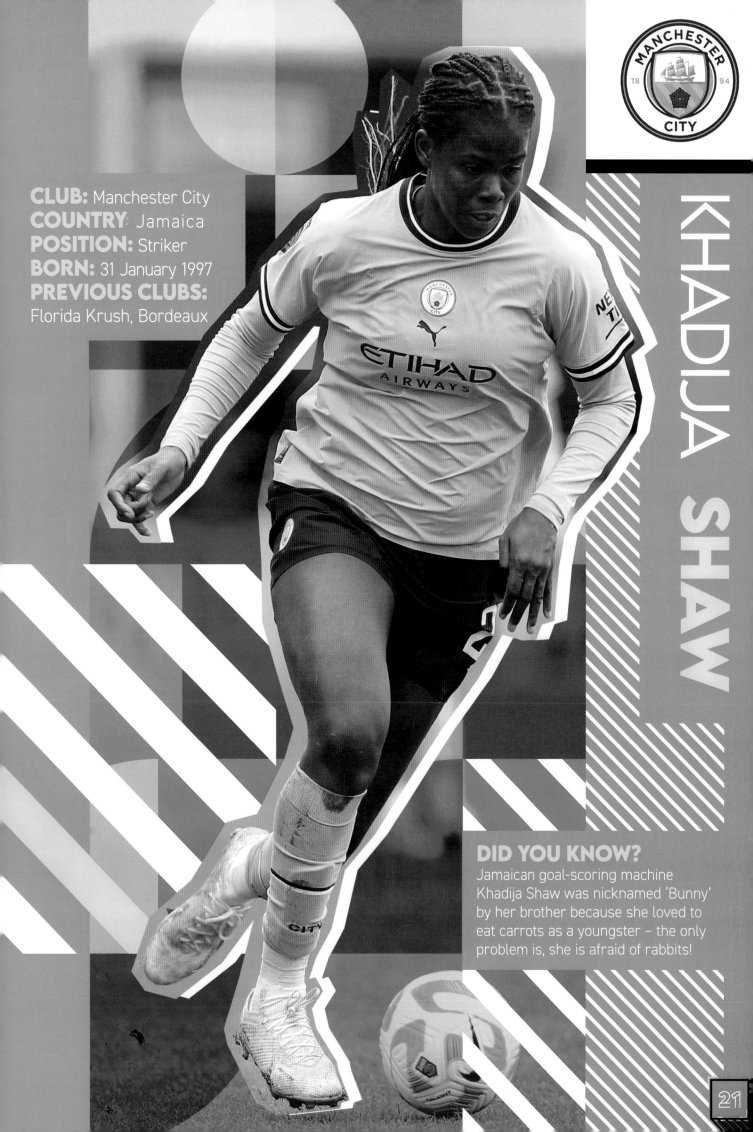

CLUB: Manchester City
COUNTRY: Jamaica
POSITION: Striker
BORN: 31 January 1997
PREVIOUS CLUBS:
Florida Krush, Bordeaux

KHADIJA SHAW

DID YOU KNOW?

Jamaican goal-scoring machine Khadija Shaw was nicknamed 'Bunny' by her brother because she loved to eat carrots as a youngster – the only problem is, she is afraid of rabbits!

21

WORLD CLUB

WORDSEARCH

MONACO

REAL SOCIEDAD

BAYERN MUNICH

MANCHESTER UNITED

LIVERPOOL

INTER MILAN

ANDERLECHT

BARCELONA

BENFICA

DYNAMO KYIV

ARSENAL

RIVER PLATE

REAL MADRID

JUVENTUS

OLYMPIACOS

RED BULL LEIPZIG

WOLFSBURG

PORTO

AJAX

CELTIC

TOP TIP
SOME OF COUNTRIES HAVE MORE THAN ONE TEAM IN THE LIST

ENGLAND	FRANCE	PORTUGAL	ARGENTINA
SCOTLAND	GERMANY	UKRAINE	NETHERLANDS
SPAIN	ITALY	BELGIUM	GREECE

22

Can you spot all 20 teams from around the world in the grid? And for an extra-time challenge, can you match them up to the country they play in?

G	B	E	D	S	I	I	A	X	S	K	F	D	R	X	B	T	N
I	L	T	V	D	X	N	T	Y	P	R	F	A	I	K	M	H	X
Z	N	X	Q	Y	U	T	Q	F	E	Z	Q	D	V	H	W	C	R
P	O	R	T	O	F	E	D	A	L	R	E	E	E	Q	T	E	J
I	U	M	J	C	R	R	L	J	D	G	U	I	R	N	S	L	N
E	J	L	N	F	E	M	O	J	R	P	H	C	P	C	T	R	G
L	U	O	F	F	A	I	B	Z	M	C	B	O	L	B	M	E	D
L	U	E	I	D	F	L	I	E	I	E	I	S	A	Z	P	D	S
L	Y	M	R	I	N	A	P	N	N	E	K	L	T	A	O	N	O
U	X	I	F	A	I	N	U	F	X	R	J	A	E	Z	Y	A	D
B	D	U	O	L	K	M	I	S	U	T	N	E	V	U	J	M	Y
D	N	N	B	C	N	C	N	D	F	K	V	R	F	P	T	Y	N
E	Q	S	V	R	A	M	L	V	I	Y	K	O	M	A	N	Y	D
R	I	F	E	F	V	N	Y	I	V	D	Q	E	N	V	D	N	C
W	Y	Y	B	I	B	X	O	F	V	S	K	O	B	G	C	D	F
W	A	E	Z	M	V	P	W	M	T	E	L	E	R	Q	Y	E	X
B	L	M	A	N	C	H	E	S	T	E	R	U	N	I	T	E	D
E	U	A	L	K	I	I	M	J	C	Q	B	P	F	F	U	U	X
I	X	Y	N	S	H	I	U	R	T	S	U	V	O	J	M	P	C
Z	S	G	X	E	G	C	A	W	F	A	R	F	I	O	N	W	E
A	L	H	W	N	S	B	W	L	F	P	C	S	L	A	L	Y	L
K	J	Z	W	X	N	R	O	L	Y	M	P	I	A	C	O	S	T
V	H	A	R	D	D	W	A	R	U	M	M	P	A	H	J	W	I
M	O	O	X	H	B	A	S	K	J	Y	Q	B	D	R	K	V	C

ANSWERS ON PAGES 76-77

23

STADIUM
MYSTERY

STADIUM 1

CAPACITY 62,850

TEAM: STADIUM:

STADIUM 2

CAPACITY 61,015

TEAM: STADIUM:

STADIUM 3

CAPACITY 56,000

TEAM: STADIUM:

OFFICIAL SUPPORTERS CLUBS

YOU'LL NEVER WALK ALONE

This is the ultimate test of your football knowledge! Using a variety of images, snippets and clues, there are six stadium mysteries to solve. Can you guess the identity of these Premier League grounds?

STADIUM 4

CAPACITY
25,700

TEAM: STADIUM:

STADIUM 5

CAPACITY
60,704

TEAM: STADIUM:

STADIUM 6

CAPACITY
52,305

TEAM: STADIUM:

ANSWERS ON PAGES 76-77

SHOOT'S SUPER QUIZ

1st HALF

So, you think you know your stuff? We'll soon find out! Our two-part quiz has 40 questions in total. You'll get points for each correct question, ranging from one point to three, with 80 points available in total. When you've finished both halves of the quiz, check the answers and add up your score to see what rating you get!

1 — 3 POINTS

Which team did Mikel Arteta NOT play for? Arsenal, Manchester City or Everton?

2 — 3 POINTS

England international Rachel Daly plays for which FA Women's Super League club?

3 — 2 POINTS

Who play their home games at Kenilworth Road? Luton Town, Watford or Reading?

4 — 2 POINTS

True or false? Barcelona have won the Champions League more than Bayern Munich.

5 — 1 POINT

Whose club badge is this?

6 — 1 POINT

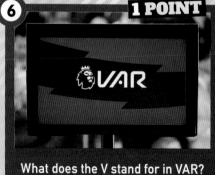

What does the V stand for in VAR? Virtual, Video or Vision?

7 — 2 POINTS

Which club plays at the Amex Stadium?

8 — 2 POINTS

Hollywood actor Ryan Reynolds is co-owner of which Welsh club?

26

9 — **3 POINTS**

Who is this international manager?

....

10 — **2 POINTS**

Are Sheffield United nicknamed 'The Swords', 'The Steels' or 'The Blades'?

....

11 — **2 POINTS**

Which Red Devil does his tattoo belong to. Clue, it's the letter 'F'.

....

12 — **2 POINTS**

True or false? Kevin De Bruyne and Mo Salah both played for Chelsea.

....

13 — **1 POINT**

Which club does England keeper Mary Earps play for?

....

14 — **1 POINT**

Whose fans are known as the 'Toon Army'?

....

15 — **2 POINTS**

Which Premier League club has a bubble machine blowing bubbles before each home game?

....

16 — **1 POINT**

Which Premier League club did Burnley boss Vincent Kompany once play for?

....

17 — **2 POINTS**

Who is this experienced manager? Roy Hodgson or Neil Warnock?

....

18 — **3 POINTS**

Which country does forward Caroline Weir represent?

....

19 — **3 POINTS**

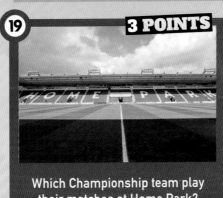

Which Championship team play their matches at Home Park?

....

20 — **2 POINTS**

True or False? Liverpool striker Diogo Jota plays international football for Spain.

....

ANSWERS ON PAGES 76-77

THE AMERICAN DREAM TEAM

Lionel Messi's joined Inter Miami during the summer of 2023 – the biggest move yet by a top player from a European club – but there have been others. Here are some star names who have gone to the USA towards the end of a glorious career...

In 2018, the Swedish superstar left Manchester United to join LA Galaxy. The striker has enjoyed a long, glorious career with clubs such as Barcelona, PSG, Inter Milan and AC Milan, but he thoroughly enjoyed his two seasons in the Major League Soccer (MLS), playing 58 games and scoring 53 goals.

ZLATAN IBRAHIMOVIC
LA GALAXY

The Arsenal legend surprised the football world when he moved to the MLS in 2010. Henry left the Gunners to join Barcelona before enjoying more than four rewarding seasons with New York Red Bulls. Henry would play 135 games and score 52 goals and made a huge impact on youngsters throughout the US during his time Stateside.

THIERRY HENRY
NEW YORK RED BULLS

GIORGIO CHIELLINI
LOS ANGELES FC

This defensive giant spent 18 years with Juventus before deciding to try his luck in the MLS with Los Angeles FC in 2022. Having played more than 500 games for Juventus and earned 117 caps for Italy, it's hard to think of a more experienced defender in world football, though injuries have hampered his time in California.

Another major signing for Los Angeles FC, Gareth Bale moved from Real Madrid in 2022 for one last year before retiring from the game. The Wales legend, who made his name with Tottenham before moving to the Bernabeu, spent nine years with the La Liga giants where he won five Champions League titles. Though he had a loan year back with Spurs, he ended a glittering career in LA.

GARETH BALE
LOS ANGELES FC

Former England captain Wayne Rooney followed a similar path to Gareth Bale in that he played many years for one club, returned to his boyhood club for one season before jetting off to the MLS. Manchester United legend Rooney won everything imaginable with the Reds during his 13 years at Old Trafford, earning 120 England caps along the way. He had one season with his first club Everton but then joined DC United for two seasons in 2018. In 2022, he returned to manage DC United.

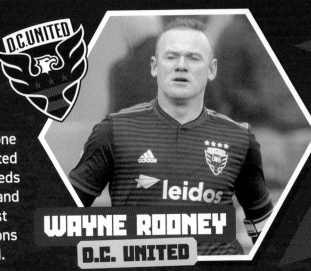

WAYNE ROONEY
D.C. UNITED

ANDREA PIRLO
NEW YORK CITY FC

Serie A legend Andrea Pirlo decided he would end his career with the newly-formed New York City FC in 2015. The gifted playmaker had carved his career out with AC Milan and Juventus over a 14-year career and is regarded as one of Italy's greatest players. Winner of 116 Italy caps, Pirlo's three seasons with NYCFC saw him make 62 appearances and help lift the MLS profile even higher.

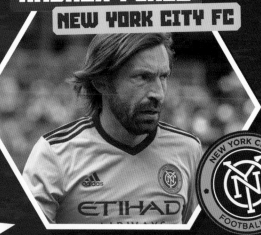

DAVID BECKHAM LA GALAXY

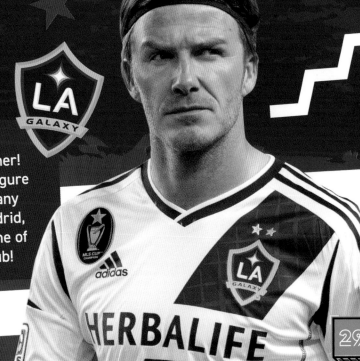

One of the most famous faces to join the MLS, David Beckham and the USA were made for each other! In many ways, 'Becks' has been the most important figure in helping the MLS establish itself globally. After many glorious years with Manchester United and Real Madrid, Beckham signed for LA Galaxy in 2007 and is now one of the owners of Inter Miami – Lionel Messi's new club!

GUESS WHO?

Can you guess the identity of these Premier League players below? We've given you three clues to help solve the mystery...

Player 1

CLUE 1:
A real Jack in the box

CLUE 2:
You'd recognise those calves anywhere!

CLUE 3:
Wears the No.10 shirt

Player 2

CLUE 1:
He's a top Gunner

CLUE 2:
Likes to play on the right wing

CLUE 3:
Lucky number 7

Player 3

CLUE 1:
A Merseyside Messiah!

CLUE 2:
Comes from the land of the Pyramids

CLUE 3:
Wears the No.11 shirt

Player 4

CLUE 1:
Part of the Toon Army!

CLUE 2:
Played for Coventry and Bournemouth

CLUE 3:
Wears the No.9 shirt

ANSWERS ON PAGES 76-77

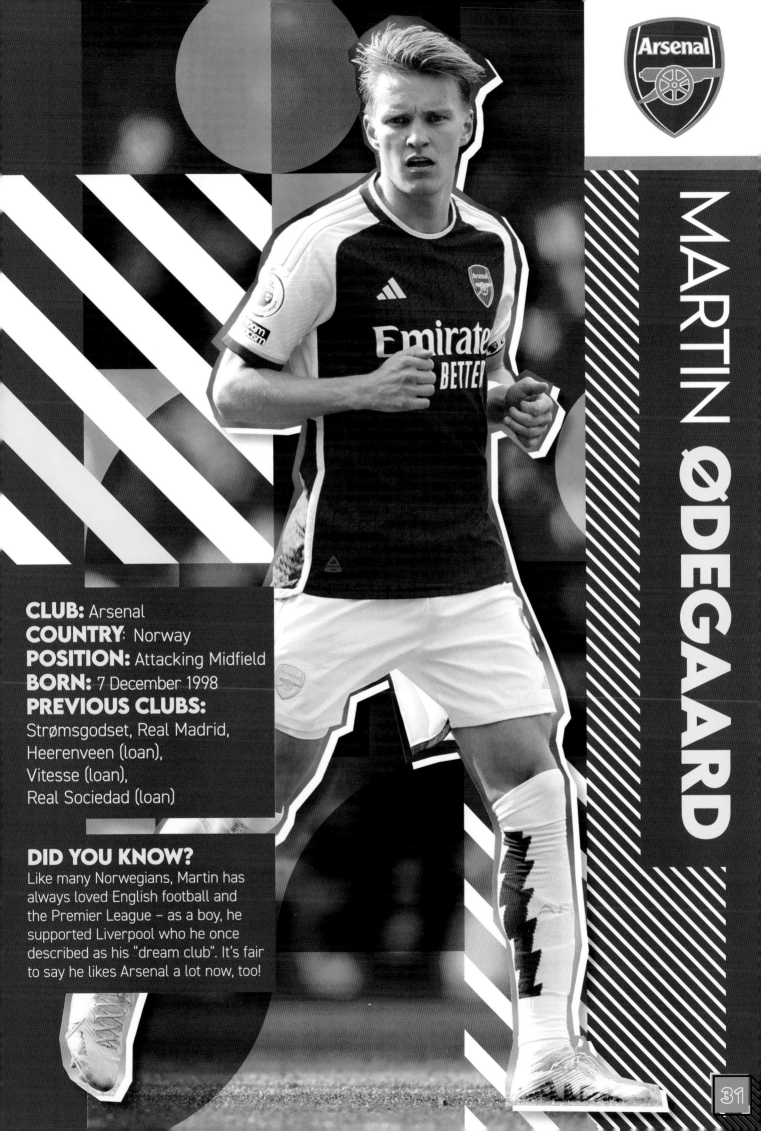

MARTIN ØDEGAARD

CLUB: Arsenal
COUNTRY: Norway
POSITION: Attacking Midfield
BORN: 7 December 1998
PREVIOUS CLUBS:
Strømsgodset, Real Madrid,
Heerenveen (loan),
Vitesse (loan),
Real Sociedad (loan)

DID YOU KNOW?
Like many Norwegians, Martin has always loved English football and the Premier League – as a boy, he supported Liverpool who he once described as his "dream club". It's fair to say he likes Arsenal a lot now, too!

31

WOMEN'S SUPER LEAGUE

CHAMPIONS 2022-23

TOP STATS!

It was another thrilling season for women's football with numerous attendance records broken, a title race to the last day and emerging talent everywhere. Here are our Shoot supercharged lists for 2023!

HONOURS BOARD

Champions: Chelsea

Runners-up: Manchester United

Promoted to the WSL: Bristol City

FA Women's Cup: Chelsea

Continental Cup: Arsenal

WSL Player of the Season: Rachel Daly (Aston Villa)

WSL Manager of the Season: Emma Hayes (Chelsea)

MOST GOALS SCORED (TEAM)

Chelsea 66 goals

Manchester United 56 goals

Manchester City 50 goals

Arsenal 49 goals

Aston Villa 47 goals

MOST GOALS CONCEDED (TEAM)

Brighton & Hove Albion 63 goals

Reading 57 goals

Leicester City 48 goals

Tottenham Hotspur 47 goals

West Ham United 44 goals

MOST GOALS SCORED (PLAYER)

Rachel Daly
(Aston Villa) 22 goals

Khadija Shaw
(Man City) 20 goals

Bethany England
(Spurs) 14 goals

Sam Kerr
(Chelsea) 12 goals

Leah Galton
Alessia Russo
(Man Utd) 10 goals

MOST ASSISTS

Guro Reiten (Chelsea)
11 assists

Ona Batlle (Man Utd)
Kirsty Hanson (Aston Villa)
Chloe Kelly (Man City)
9 assists

Kenza Dali (Aston Villa)
Ella Toone (Man Utd)
Katie Zelem (Man Utd)
5 assists

TOP 5 CROWDS

47,367 Arsenal 4-0 Spurs

46,881 Arsenal 1-1 Chelsea

44,259 Man City 1-1 Man United

40,064 Arsenal 2-3 Man United

38,35 Chelsea 3-0 Spurs

CLEAN SHEETS

Mary Earps (Man United)
14 clean sheets

Manuela Zinsberger (Arsenal)
10 clean sheets

Ann-Katrin Berger (Chelsea)
8 clean sheets

Mackenzie Arnold (West Ham)
Hannah Hampton (Aston Villa)
Janina Leitzig (Leicester City)
Ellie Roebuck (Man City)
5 clean sheets

+ASSIST KINGS

They don't always get the headlines, but their role is vital! So, who made more Premier League goals than anyone else? Here are the best playmakers from 2022/23!

KEVIN DE BRUYNE

16 2022/23 PL ASSISTS

No surprise to see the Belgian maestro in this group. 'KDB' reached the 100 Premier League assists milestone in 2022/23 and will surely add many more to this in 2024.

MO SALAH

12 2022/23 PL ASSISTS

Mo Salah doesn't just score plenty of goals – he makes them, too. The Egyptian forward chipped in with 12 during 2022/23 and has a total of 59 Premier League assists.

LEANDRO TROSSARD

12 2022/23 PL ASSISTS

Leandro switched clubs halfway through the season and still managed to keep his assist ratio high. His 12 assists in the season put him level with Mo Salah.

MICHAEL OLISE

11 2022/23 PL ASSISTS

The exciting winger managed to top team-mate Wilfried Zaha in 2022/23 with 11 Premier League assists. Not bad when you consider Palace only scored 40 goals all season!

BUKAYO SAKA

11 2022/23 PL ASSISTS

The England and Arsenal winger enjoyed another fantastic season – his 11 Premier League assists ensured Arsenal stayed in the Premier League title race almost to the finish.

RIYAD MAHREZ

10 2022/23 PL ASSISTS

The Premier League champions provide more than one player in our assist kings list which is impressive as Mahrez wasn't a regular starter for City in 2022/23. He has 61 in total for City and Leicester.

SUPER HANDS

Every good team needs a safe pair of hands between the sticks! So, who had more Premier League clean sheets than anyone else? Here are the best shot stoppers from 2022/23!

DAVID DE GEA

17
2022/23 PL
CLEAN SHEETS

His 17 clean sheets for the Reds allowed him to claim his second Premier League Golden Glove award. Despite his length of time in England, he's still only 32 going into the new season and has many more years at the top left.

ALISSON BECKER

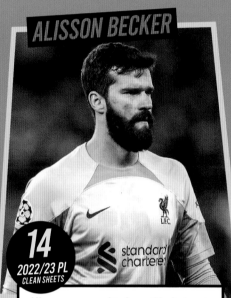

14
2022/23 PL
CLEAN SHEETS

Alisson managed to keep 14 shut-outs despite a poor Liverpool campaign. That's a pretty decent return from the 37 games he played and proof he is one of the best in the world.

NICK POPE

14
2022/23 PL
CLEAN SHEETS

Pope couldn't have had a better first season at St James' Park – dependable and consistent throughout, he is one of the main reasons the Magpies achieved Champions League qualification.

AARON RAMSDALE

14
2022/23 PL
CLEAN SHEETS

With 14 shut-outs, Arsenal's Aaron Ramsdale was in contention for the Golden Glove until the Gunners' late season wobble – he is sure to challenge again in 2023/24.

DAVID RAYA

12
2022/23 PL
CLEAN SHEETS

Brentford maintained their Premier League status for another season with ease, and their Spanish shot-stopper kept 12 clean sheets along the way including shut-outs against both Manchester City and United as well as Chelsea home and away!

EDERSON

11
2022/23 PL
CLEAN SHEETS

Ederson has dominated the Golden Glove award in recent years and had won it three times in succession going into 2022/23 – yet this season, he finishes in fifth. A brilliant, innovative keeper, he'll be back again this season no doubt!

SPOT THE BALL

Six balls have mysteriously appeared in each of these action shots below. Can you work out which is the real one?

GAME 1

CHELSEA V NOTTINGHAM FOREST

GAME 2

BRENTFORD V WEST HAM UNITED

GAME 3
MANCHESTER CITY V CHELSEA

GAME 4
LIVERPOOL V BOURNEMOUTH

ANSWERS ON PAGES 76-77

WORLD

Everyone loves a derby match! That often means two teams from the same geographical area. But not always, as you will see below! We've chosen 8 of the fiercest derby matches in world football and marked them in different categories.

GLASGOW

RANGERS v CELTIC

There's no love lost between these two Scottish giants! The atmosphere is always electric whether it is at Celtic Park or Ibrox, this is always an explosive contest on or off the pitch!

SHOOT RATINGS
Passion: 10/10
Global appeal: 5/10
History: 9/10
TOTAL: 24/30

MANCHESTER

CITY v UNITED

The battle of Manchester, Blues v Reds... this is a game that can define a season and has been that way for more than 120 years. A fierce city rivalry that often bubbles over on the pitch, this is a huge game!

SHOOT RATINGS
Passion: 9/10
Global appeal: 8/10
History: 9/10
TOTAL: 26/30

ARGENTINA

RIVER PLATE v BOCA JUNIORS

When two of Argentina's top sides meet, there are always fireworks! The Buenos Aires derby is known as the 'Superclasico' and history suggests the players and fans don't like each other that much!

SHOOT RATINGS
Passion: 9/10
Global appeal: 8/10
History: 10/10
TOTAL: 27/30

SPAIN

REAL MADRID v BARCELONA

El Clasico — the biggest game in Spanish football, though it is not a classic city derby. In fact, the two cities are many miles apart, but their dominance of La Liga has made this a derby of sorts!

SHOOT RATINGS
Passion: 10/10
Global appeal: 4/10
History: 10/10
TOTAL: 24/30

DERBIES

ARSENAL v SPURS

With neither side winning many trophies in the past decade, this North London derby has lost a little bit of its edge — but when there is a lot at stake, it can certainly hit the heights of seasons gone by!

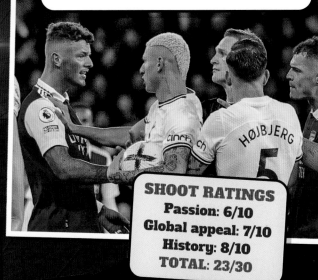

SHOOT RATINGS
Passion: 6/10
Global appeal: 7/10
History: 8/10
TOTAL: 23/30

MERSEYSIDE

LIVERPOOL v EVERTON

Like Manchester, it's Blues versus Reds with only Stanley Park separating these two Merseyside giants. Everton will move to a new stadium in 2024/25, but it's unlikely to replicate the Goodison Park or Anfield atmospheres.

SHOOT RATINGS
Passion: 8/10
Global appeal: 8/10
History: 9/10
TOTAL: 25/30

ITALY

MILAN v INTER

Known as the Derby della Madonnina, the two Milan giants are almost unique in that, while they are fierce rivals, they share the same stadium, the San Siro! Does that take anything away from these derby games? Not a chance!

NORTH-EAST

NEWCASTLE v SUNDERLAND

Two cities defined by the rivers that run through them — known as the Tyne and the Wear derby. Separated by about 30 miles, these two clubs don't play each other that much of late, but when they do, it's a game you wouldn't want to miss.

SHOOT RATINGS
Passion: 10/10
Global appeal: 7/10
History: 8/10
TOTAL: 25/30

SHOOT RATINGS
Passion: 9/10
Global appeal: 7/10
History: 9/10
TOTAL: 25/30

DID YOU

Want to impress your friends with your knowledge of the game? Just memorise these facts and stats and reel them off and watch their jaws drop!

West Ham United's 2-1 win over Fiorentina in the Europa Conference final was the Hammers' first major trophy since they won the FA Cup in 1980 – 43 years ago!

Barcelona versus Scottish Premiership side **Dundee United** – only one winner, right? Well, that's correct because the clubs have met four times in Europe and Dundee United have won all four! They beat the Catalans home and away in 1966-67 and again in 1986-87, a 100% record no other British side can match.

A defender who doesn't make a foul? We are talking about German legend **Philipp Lahm**, here! He went an entire year between September 2014 to October 2015 without committing a single foul – proof that if you time your tackles right, there's no need to foul. Lahm was a superb player for Bayern Munich and Germany, and he was never once red carded.

Pep Guardiola once had a brief trial with Manchester City towards the end of his playing career – but both the player and club decided to go their separate ways after the week-long trial in 2005.

KNOW?

We all love entertaining football, but **AC Milan** appear to have won the 1993-94 Serie A title playing exactly the opposite! They scored just 36 goals in 34 games, winning nine games 1-0 and drawing seven 0-0 – a defensive masterclass but a bit boring!

Manchester City may have won the Champions League in 2023 with a 1-0 win over Inter Milan, but the club's first European trophy came 53 years earlier in 1970 when they beat Polish side Gornik Zabrze 2-1 in the European Cup Winners' Cup final.

Want an out of this world stat? What do Arsenal's legendary boss **Arsene Wenger**, former Barcelona coach and player **Johan Cruyff** and Chelsea and Germany star **Michael Ballack** all have in common? The answer is they each have an asteroid named after them! 33179 Arsenewenger, 14282 Cruyff and 79647 Ballack are all presumably flying through space as we speak!

Former Celtic and current Spurs boss **Angelos Postecoglou** has managed teams in five different countries, Greece, Australia, Japan, Scotland and now England!

2023 WINNERS

This year has seen loads of awesome champions crowned. Take a look back at the winners from around the world, plus you can fill in the blanks. It's trophy time!

DOMESTIC

PREMIER LEAGUE & FA CUP
MANCHESTER CITY

EFL CUP
MANCHESTER UNITED

CHAMPIONSHIP
BURNLEY

Promoted
Sheffield United,
Luton Town (play-offs)

LEAGUE ONE
PLYMOUTH ARGYLE

Promoted
Ipswich Town, Sheffield
Wednesday (play-offs)

LEAGUE TWO
LEYTON ORIENT

Promoted
Stevenage, Northampton
Carlisle (play-offs)

NATIONAL LEAGUE
1st: Wrexham
Promoted: Notts County

SCOTTISH PREMIERSHIP
Celtic

SCOTTISH CUP
Celtic

SCOTTISH LEAGUE CUP
Celtic

NIFL PREMIERSHIP
Larn

CYMRU PREMIER
The New Saints

COMMUNITY SHIELD
....

EUROPE

LA LIGA (Spain)
1st: Barcelona
2nd: Real Madrid

BUNDESLIGA (Germany)
1st: Bayern Munich
2nd: Borussia Dortmund

LIGUE 1 (France)
1st: Paris Saint-Germain
2nd: Lens

SERIE A (Italy)
1st: Napoli
2nd: Lazio

EREDIVISIE (Netherlands)
1st: Feyenoord
2nd: PSV Eindhoven

PRIMEIRA LIGA (Portugal)
1st: Benfica
2nd: Porto

CHAMPIONS LEAGUE
MANCHESTER CITY

EUROPA LEAGUE
SEVILLA

EUROPA CONFERENCE
WEST HAM UNITED

WOMEN

WSL & FA CUP
WINNERS 2023
CHELSEA

UEFA SUPER CUP
....

INTERNATIONAL

UEFA NATIONS LEAGUE
....

FIFA CLUB WORLD CUP
....

WOMEN'S WORLD CUP
....

LEAGUE CUP
ARSENAL

CHAMPIONS LEAGUE
BARCELONA

CHAMPIONSHIP
1st: Bristol City

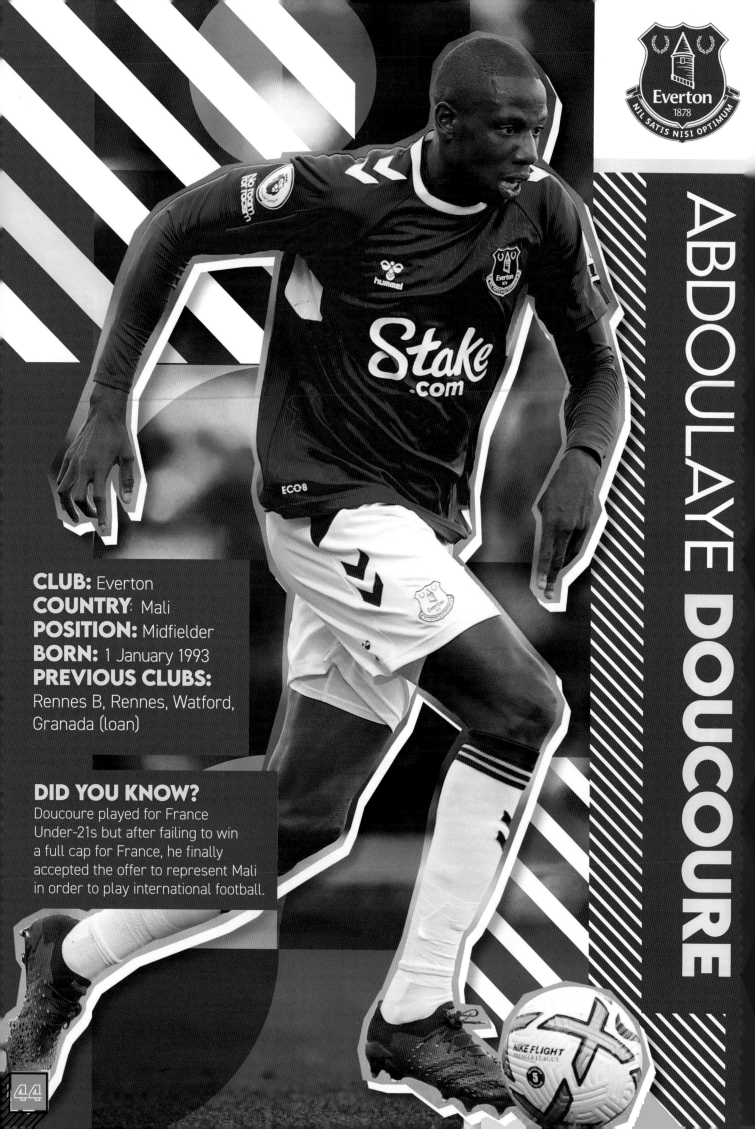

ABDOULAYE DOUCOURE

CLUB: Everton
COUNTRY: Mali
POSITION: Midfielder
BORN: 1 January 1993
PREVIOUS CLUBS:
Rennes B, Rennes, Watford,
Granada (loan)

DID YOU KNOW?
Doucoure played for France
Under-21s but after failing to win
a full cap for France, he finally
accepted the offer to represent Mali
in order to play international football.

CLUB: Liverpool
COUNTRY: England
POSITION: Wing/Midfield
BORN: 4 April 2003
PREVIOUS CLUBS:
Fulham,
Blackburn Rovers (loan)

HARVEY ELLIOTT

DID YOU KNOW?
In May 2019 he made his Premier League debut against Wolves aged 16 years and 30 days and - at the time - became the youngest player to play a Premier League game.

45

ELLA TOONE >

SHOOT sat down for a chat with one of the brightest stars in the FA Women's Super League...

Ella, how do you see yourself?

"I was once a little girl with a lot of dreams, and I have just managed to achieve them."

Who was your inspiration?

"I used to love watching Cristiano Ronaldo and I'd just sit there on my laptop and Google 'Cristiano Ronaldo skills' and then go out in the back garden and try to practice them."

What's the best thing about being a Manchester United player?

"Growing up a Manchester United fan and then being able to play for the club you love and support week in, week out, is really special."

What's it like seeing kids with your name on the back of their shirt?

"It just feels really weird when I see that or if I hear my name being chanted as well because I'll always be just Ella and I know where I came from and where my roots are. I'm just a Tyldesley girl."

You began with United's academy but had to leave for Blackburn and Manchester City – how did that come about?

"There was no Manchester United women's team back then and nothing to strive for, so I had to make the decision to leave. I was at Blackburn Rovers first and then signed a dual contract with Manchester City. When you turn 18, that's when you are offered a professional contract, but that didn't happen for me. It was really hard at the time. I sat and cried in a Starbucks for about an hour with my dad and my agent, but looking back, it's probably the best thing that could have happened because it made me focus and work ever harder."

But you went back to United eventually...?

"There were rumours Manchester United were starting a women's team so when the manager Casey Stoney called my agent to see if I was interested, I nearly bit her hand off! It was Manchester United, my team and my home and I knew they believed in me, and my ambitions matched theirs and I've been happy ever since."

What do you bring to the Lionesses team and what was it like winning the Euros and scoring THAT goal?

"I bring hard work, bravery, play with freedom and hopefully I can score a lot of goals, too! I don't think we'll ever get bored of hearing 'European Champions'. It was an unbelievable summer that we had together, and I think we'll want to keep remembering it every single day. That will never get old. Scoring in the final was the best feeling I've ever had, and it was an unbelievable moment and very special."

What are your ambitions?

"I want to win everything! I want to win things for myself, like the Ballon D'Or – why not set those targets? This is just the beginning."

What advice would you give young players hoping to follow in your footsteps?

"Enjoy every minute of it. Now I've learnt so much more, I think that you've just got to be that little kid who used to play on the street and in the park and just go out there and express yourself in different ways. Just enjoy yourself and be confident and believe in yourself. Make sure that you set yourself some dreams because you can achieve them."

FACT FILE

CLUB: Manchester United
COUNTRY: England
POSITION: Forward
BORN: 2 September 1999
BIRTHPLACE: Tyldesley, Manchester
PREVIOUS CLUBS: Blackburn Rovers, Manchester City

SOCIAL SCENE

Social media is a way for fans, to see what their favourite stars get up to when they step off the pitch. Some players post pictures that can get millions of likes – so here Shoot's run-down of the footballers who have the most followers in Insta!

Credit: @cristiano

Credit: @leomessi

Credit: @neymarjr

Credit: @k.mbappe

Credit: @davidbeckham

Credit: @ronaldinho

CRISTIANO RONALDO
@cristiano
589 million followers

LIONEL MESSI
@leomessi
471 million followers

NEYMAR JR
@neymarjr
209 million followers

KYLIAN MBAPPÉ
@k.mbappe
104 million followers

DAVID BECKHAM
@davidbeckham
79.8 million followers

RONALDINHO
@ronaldinho
73.4 million followers

MARCELO VIEIRA
@marcelotwelve
64 million followers

ZLATAN IBRAHIMOVIC
@iamzlatanibrahimovic
60.5 million followers

Follower figures correct as of 1st June 2023

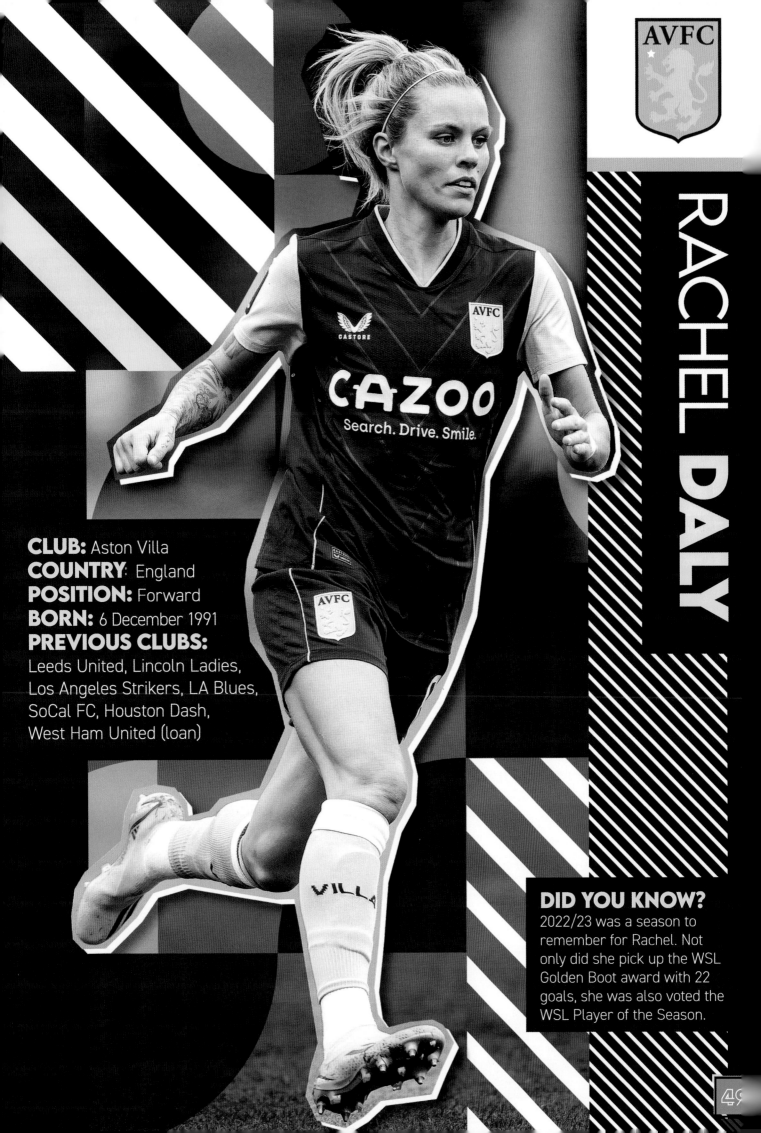

AVFC

RACHEL DALY

CLUB: Aston Villa
COUNTRY: England
POSITION: Forward
BORN: 6 December 1991
PREVIOUS CLUBS:
Leeds United, Lincoln Ladies,
Los Angeles Strikers, LA Blues,
SoCal FC, Houston Dash,
West Ham United (loan)

DID YOU KNOW?
2022/23 was a season to remember for Rachel. Not only did she pick up the WSL Golden Boot award with 22 goals, she was also voted the WSL Player of the Season.

KYLIAN MBAPPE

The France forward has it all. Pace to burn, lightning fast acceleration, stamina, and strength – he's also a great finisher and has good versatility. Any team with Mbappe in their starting XI is a team to be feared and, guess what? He is only going to get better!

SHOOT VALUATION £250 MILLION

YOUR VALUATION £ ....

VINICIUS JUNIOR

Brazilian winger Vinicius Junior has established himself as one of football's top talents. A tireless worker for the team, he is a skilful winger with a fast turn of pace. His speed can leave even the quickest of defenders chasing shadows.

SHOOT VALUATION £175 MILLION

YOUR VALUATION £ ....

BUKAYO SAKA

Bukayo Saka is yet another talented English player with the world at his feet. A tricky right winger, Saka can dribble, beat full-backs with his impressive pace and score fantastic goals. A huge player for Arsenal and England, Saka is only going to get better and better.

SHOOT VALUATION £120 MILLION

YOUR VALUATION £ ....

ERLING HAALAND

The Man City goal machine broke all kinds of records in his first Premier League season. A phenomenal talent in world football, with his agility, pace and size. Agile, strong, and equally good in the air and on the ground, he could become the greatest striker of all time.

SHOOT VALUATION £235 MILLION

YOUR VALUATION £ ....

JUDE BELLINGHAM

Bellingham is arguably one of the most complete midfielders in European football. Still very young, he has plenty of experience in a short space of time and is very much a modern player. He has excellent technique, can run for 90 minutes, and has a wonderful array of passes in his locker.

SHOOT VALUATION £125 MILLION

YOUR VALUATION £ ....

CLUB

VICTOR OSIMHEN

This powerhouse of a striker has become one of Europe's most sought-after forwards. It looked like he would be no more than a journeyman footballer, but after a successful spell at Lille, he fulfilled his potential at Napoli where his strength, hold-up play, and aerial prowess set him apart from his peers.

SHOOT VALUATION £115 MILLION

YOUR VALUATION £

PHIL FODEN

Man City and England's box-of-tricks, local her Phil Foden has six seasons under his belt already. Skilful, an excellent dribbler and with a wonderful eye for a pass and spectacular goal, Foden gets people off their seats and is almost unique in English football.

SHOOT VALUATION £110 MILLION

YOUR VALUATION £

JAMAL MUSIALA

An exceptional talent, the versatile attacking midfielder can play on either wing or through the middle with his dribbling ability among the best in Europe. Balanced and agile and already a full international for Germany, Musiala can become a huge player for club and country.

SHOOT VALUATION £100 MILLION

YOUR VALUATION £

INVITATION TO THE £100M CLUB

HERE IS YOUR CHANCE TO NAME FIVE MORE PLAYERS YOU THINK ARE WORTHY OF THIS EXCLUSIVE CLUB. PUT YOUR SELECTIONS AND VALUATION BELOW AND SEE IF ANY HAPPEN DURING THIS SEASON – OR BEYOND!

THE ULTIMATE CHAMPIONS LEAGUE QUIZ

Everybody loves the Champions League, but how good is YOUR knowledge? Test your ability with our supercharged Champions League quiz and see how you get on!

1

Which club has won the most Champions League titles?

....

2

Which club has had more appearances in the Champions League – Bayern Munich or Benfica?

....

3

Who has played more Champions League matches – Basel or Manchester City?

....

4

True or false? PSG have never won the Champions League.

....

5

Who has more Champions League assists – Lionel Messi or Cristiano Ronaldo?

....

6

Who has the most Champions League goals – Cristiano Ronaldo or Lionel Messi?

....

7

How many Champions League penalties has Robert Lewandowski scored? 10, 14 or 16?

....

8

True or false? Arsenal are the only English side to win the Women's Champions League.

9

Karim Benzema scored the most Champions League goals in one season – but how many did he get? Was it 15, 16 or 17 goals?

....

10

How many Champions League red cards has Sergio Ramos received? Is it 4, 6 or 10 red cards?

....

11

Which player scored five goals in one game against RB Leipzig during the 2022/23 season?

....

12

What was the Champions League originally called?

....

13

Which of these English teams has NOT won the European Cup/ Champions League? Nottingham Forest, Aston Villa or Leeds United?

....

14

True or false? England is the only nation to win the competition six years in a row.

....

15

True or false? Both Scottish giants Celtic and Rangers have won the competition.

....

16

Which city has more Champions League wins? Milan, London or Amsterdam?

....

17

The most successful Champions League manager is Carlo Ancelotti – but how many times has he won the competition? 3, 4 or 5?

....

18

Real Madrid have won in 14 finals – but how many times have they lost the final? Is it 3, 4 or 5?

....

19

Manchester City won the 2023 Champions League, but who scored the only goal in the final?

....

20

Who did Barcelona beat to win the 2023 Women's Champions League?

....

SPOT THE DIFFERENCE

Look closely at Picture A and Picture B – they're the same, right?
Wrong! There are TEN differences in Picture B – the question is,
can you spot them all? Circle the ones you find.

A

B

1 2 3 4 5 6 7 8 9 10

54

ANSWERS ON PAGES 76-77

ANTONY

CLUB: Manchester United
COUNTRY: Brazil
POSITION: Right Wing
BORN: 24 February 2000
PREVIOUS CLUBS:
Sao Paolo, Ajax

DID YOU KNOW?

Antony grew up in a 'favela' in Sao Paolo, Brazil. A favela is a densely populated ghetto, inhabited mainly by working class families who live in cramped conditions with very few amenities. He played football in the streets and also loved to play futsal.

HARRY KANE

Harry Kane became England's all-time leading goalscorer when his strike in the Euro 2024 qualifier against Italy saw him surpass the previous record-holder, Wayne Rooney. Shoot takes a look through his record breaking Three-Lions journey!

Kane was first named in the senior England squad on 19 March 2015 when then manager Roy Hodgson included him in the games against Lithuania and Italy.

It took Kane just 80 seconds to score on his England debut! After replacing Wayne Rooney, Kane headed home Raheem Sterling's cross against Lithuania at Wembley – the perfect start for the future skipper!

On 22 May 2016, Kane took his first England penalty – and missed! It was the first time in six years an England player had missed a spot-kick and his wayward spot-kick meant he also became the first England player to completely miss the target for 10 years!

Kane first captained England on 10 June 2017 in a feisty 2018 World Cup qualifier against Scotland at Hampden Park – he scored in added time to earn England a 2-2 draw to cement his place as the nation's leader.

Kane's first hat-trick came in the 2018 World Cup finals clash with Panama which saw the Three Lions romp home 6-1 – in doing so, Kane matched the feats of Geoff Hurst (1966) and Gary Lineker (1986) by scoring a treble in a World Cup tournament.

Kane won the coveted Golden Boot at the 2018 World Cup after scoring six goals – he is only the second England player to finish top scorer at a World Cup with Gary Lineker the first to do so in 1986.

Harry captained the England side that beat Montenegro 7-0 in a Euro 2020 qualifier - it was England's 1000th game and the skipper marked with the occasion with another hat-trick!

In 2021, Harry scored 16 England goals in a calendar year, breaking his own record of 12 set two years before!

Kane became the first Englishman to score in every game during the Euro 2020 qualification campaign with 12 goals.

Against San Marino in a World Cup 2022 qualifier, Harry scored a 'perfect' hat-trick consisting of a headed goal, a, right-footed goal and a left-footed goal.

Kane has scored more penalty goals than any other England player (18 as of 01/06/2023) – he has also missed four spot-kicks, which is more than any other Three Lions player.

GOAL 54

On the 23rd March 2023, Harry Kane became England's all-time leading goalscorer with a penalty against Italy in Naples.

SHOOT'S
SUPER QUIZ

Are you ready for the 2nd half? Check your answers when you've finished, and don't forget to add your 1st half score to your 2nd half score to see how well you've done!

21 · **2 POINTS**

Which Spanish club plays at the Santiago Bernabeu?

22 · **1 POINT**

Whose club badge is this?

23 · **2 POINTS**

True or False? A referee can receive a red card and be sent off.

24 · **2 POINTS**

What's the name of the West Ham United mascot? Hammy the Hammer, Hammerhead, or Harry Hammer?

25 · **2 POINTS**

Which team is nicknamed The Foxes?

26 · **2 POINTS**

How many yards from goal is the penalty spot? Is it 12 yards, 10 yards or 8 yards?

27 · **3 POINTS**

 Vs ?

Which team would Burnley play against in the Lancashire derby?

28 · **2 POINTS**

Who is this tough tackling centre back?

29 · **1 POINT**

Which team are nicknamed 'The Toffees'? Is it West Brom, Sunderland or Everton?

30 · **2 POINTS**

What is Phil Foden's favourite hobby? Fishing, Snooker or Golf?

58

31 **2 POINTS**

True or false? Sam Allardyce once managed England.

....

32 **2 POINTS**

How many World Cups has Lionel Messi won? Is it none, one or two?

....

33 **3 POINTS**

Which club did Erik ten Hag join Manchester United from?

....

34 **2 POINTS**

Who is older, Harry Kane or Son Heung-min?

....

35 **1 POINT**

Which Italian teams badge is this?

....

36 **2 POINTS**

Who won the FA Cup final in 2007 when Wembley Stadium reopened, Manchester United or Chelsea?

....

37 **2 POINTS**

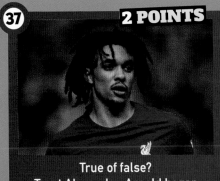

True of false? Trent Alexander-Arnold began his career with Watford.

....

38 **1 POINT**

How many goals did Kylian Mbappe score in the 2022 World Cup final against Argentina?

....

39 **3 POINTS**

Who scored England's winner in the final of the Women's Euros in 2022?

....

40 **2 POINTS**

True or False? Blackburn Rovers have won the Premier League.

....

YOUR SHOOT RATING

70-80 POINTS
You are a football genius!

60-69 POINTS
Standing ovation – great work!

50-59 POINTS
A very good effort!

40-49 POINTS
Not bad at all!

30-39 POINTS
Need to brush up a bit on your knowledge!

20-29 POINTS
Extra homework for you!

LESS THAN 20
You gave it a good try – better luck next year...

ANSWERS ON PAGES 76-77

FC BAYERN MÜNCHEN

ONE OF EUROPEAN FOOTBALL'S BRIGHTEST TALENTS...

Q: What did you want to be growing up?

"I wanted to be in the army or be a police officer – definitely one of those two – until I found out I could be a footballer! I knew I wanted to do something physical that involved being outdoors because I could never work in an office all day, typing or whatever."

Q: What do you eat before a game?

"I don't really have any superstitions, so I don't have a set meal I eat every time. I just try to stick to chicken and pasta – that has all the carbs and protein which provides fuel for you during the game."

Q: Was it difficult to leave Manchester City?

"Of course it was but I wanted to put myself in a situation where I didn't know how good I could be, and I was just ready for a change."

GEORGIA STANWAY

FACT FILE

POSITION: ATTACKING MIDFIELDER
HEIGHT: 1.62M (5FT 3IN)
BIRTH DATE: 3 JANUARY 1999
BIRTH PLACE: BARROW-IN-FURNESS
TEAMS: BAYERN MUNICH & ENGLAND

Q: What's the best piece of advice you've ever been given?

"When I was younger, I wanted everything to be perfect and to be the perfect footballer, so I put a lot of pressure on myself. I wanted to win every game, score all the time and it just wasn't realistic. You have to just control what you can control, don't put too much pressure on yourself and enjoy what you're doing. If you enjoy what you're doing, you are more likely to succeed."

Q: Are you enjoying being at Bayern Munich?

"I'm loving it. It's something I needed to do to challenge myself and I'm really happy with my decision. It feels like a family here and this is such a special environment to be part of."

Q: Best player you have played against?

"I'd probably say Wendie Renard at Lyon. I remember playing against her in the Champions League semi-final and I'd take two or three steps and she'd just be there because her legs are so long! She's so strong and powerful, she's definitely got to be up there."

Q: What in life are you most grateful for?

"I'd definitely say my family. They've contributed so much for me to get to where I am – the hours they spent taking me places, the driving, the standing watching at training sessions. They provided me with the opportunity, and I wouldn't be doing what I'm doing now if wasn't for them."

TRANSFER CHALLENGE

ANSWERS ON PAGES 76-77

Some players were signed for transfer fees that now seem remarkably low. From the six players below, guess how much they cost their club by circling the correct figure. You might be surprised at some of the bargains we've found!

FROM **TO**

CESAR AZPILICUETA

£7m £8m £9m

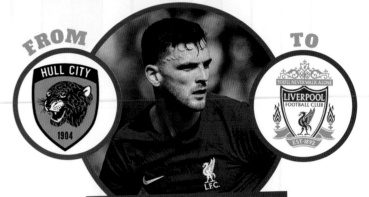

FROM **TO**

ANDREW ROBERTSON

£4m £6m £8m

FROM **TO**

SEAMUS COLEMAN

£60k £75k £100k

FROM **TO**

ILKAY GUNDOGAN

£10m £15m £20m

FROM **TO**

ALEXIS MAC ALLISTER

£3m £7m £10m

FROM **TO**

MICHAIL ANTONIO

£2m £4.5m £7m

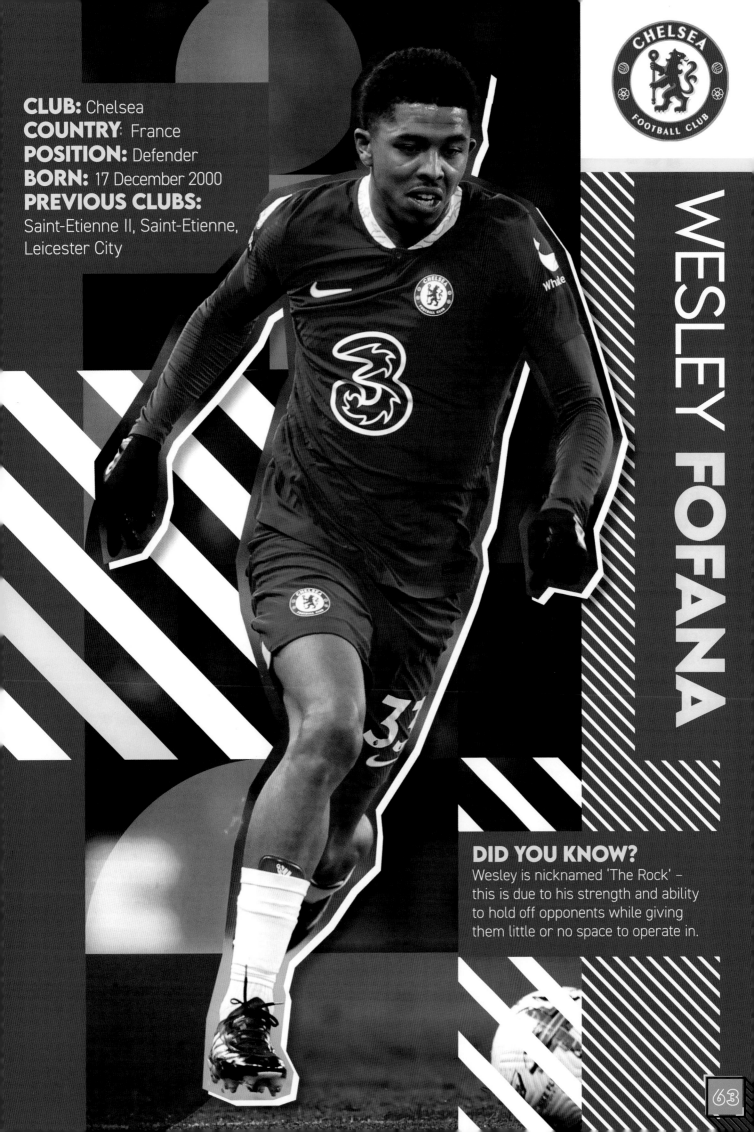

CLUB: Chelsea
COUNTRY: France
POSITION: Defender
BORN: 17 December 2000
PREVIOUS CLUBS:
Saint-Etienne II, Saint-Etienne,
Leicester City

WESLEY FOFANA

DID YOU KNOW?

Wesley is nicknamed 'The Rock' – this is due to his strength and ability to hold off opponents while giving them little or no space to operate in.

63

SHOOT'S MEN'S ULTIMATE WORLD XI

With so many fantastic footballers around the world, how do you choose just 11 players?

Shoot have chosen our Ultimate XI, with a mixture of world class talent, experience and youthful promise all blending together to form a formidable team. But there are some big names missing, too!

Below are the players who we feel deserve to be chosen – but we've left a space beneath each player for you to put your favourite stars in, just in case you don't agree with our selections.

GK

EDERSON

There is no better goalkeeper at starting play from the back than Ederson. He is super calm and can ping a 60-yard pass or play accurately through a high press to find a team-mate and start an attack. It's no wonder he's Pep's number 1!

YOUR CHOICE ....

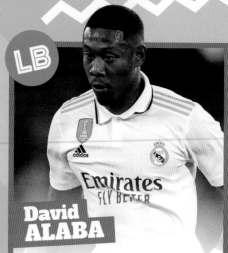

LB

David ALABA

A wonderful defender and attacking wingback who has been the best left-back in world football for a number of years. The Austrian has been a serial trophy winner throughout his career and has more than 100 caps for Austria.

YOUR CHOICE ....

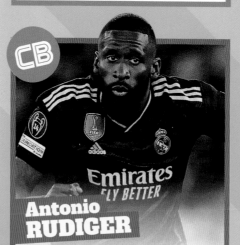

CB

Antonio RUDIGER

Tough, uncompromising and a powerhouse of a defender, Rudiger is all that and more. His wiry build and strength make him a striker's nightmare and the German will add steel to our World XI in the heart of defence.

YOUR CHOICE ....

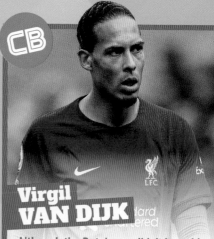

CB

Virgil VAN DIJK

Although the Dutchman didn't have his best season in a Liverpool shirt, there's no doubt that he's still one of the best. He makes the art of defending look easy as he glides across the pitch, seemingly always one step ahead of the strikers.

YOUR CHOICE ....

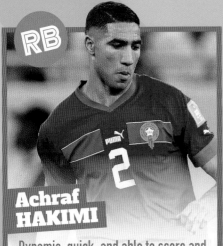

RB
Achraf HAKIMI

Dynamic, quick, and able to score and assists vital goals, he is one of the best right-back's around. And he can defend! He was outstanding as Morocco reached the World Cup semi-final in 2022 and is an excellent addition to our World XI.

YOUR CHOICE ....

MF
Joshua KIMMICH

Our holding midfielder is Bayern Munich's Joshua Kimmich. The versatile German is able to break-up play and start attacks, he has an excellent passing range as well as a mean shot. He will be our anchorman in this team.

YOUR CHOICE ....

MF
Kevin DE BRUYNE

Possibly best attacking midfielder in world football at the moment. KDB has the vision to match his passing range and sets up more goals than anyone else currently playing as well as scoring some humdingers! A genius.

YOUR CHOICE ....

MF
PEDRI

Destined for big things, Pedri is our wild card selection. The box-of-tricks attacking midfielder is capable of the unexpected, with his quick feet and technical ability, he is also the youngest member of the Shoot World XI.

YOUR CHOICE ....

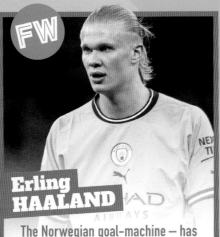

FW
Erling HAALAND

The Norwegian goal-machine — has there ever been a striker like him before? Physically powerful, fast, and intelligent with his movement, Haaland can score any type of goals and is a defender's nightmare.

YOUR CHOICE ....

FW
Kylian MBAPPE

Electric pace, power, and athleticism, the PSG main man has been one of the best forwards on the planet for several years and keeps getting better. Imagine a forward line with Mbappe and Haaland? Not bad!

YOUR CHOICE ....

FW
Vinicius JUNIOR

A superb young talent, Vinicius Junior can dribble at pace and score wonderful goals, the young Brazilian would be a handful for any defence and with Haaland central and Mbappe and Vinicius either side, this team would be pretty much unbeatable.

YOUR CHOICE

....

Do you agree? Is your favourite player included? Add your selections to the boxes below each player if you think they deserve to be part of the team.

FUTURE STAR

BRIGHTON & HOVE ALBION

One of Shoot's up and coming talents for 2023/24 is Brighton and Republic of Ireland striker Evan Ferguson – here, he answers our Q&A...

Q: Evan, what's your first football memory?

"Probably being out with my mates on the street as a kid, just kicking a ball about for fun. I was very young – maybe just four – and I've had the same next door neighbour my whole life so I just remember always being out with him."

Q: Who were your influences growing up?

"I'd probably say my dad because he was always there, taking me to training and being around when I played matches. He used to manage a team, so I was always around a football environment from a very early age."

Q: What was the first football match you attended?

"It would have been an Ireland game at the Aviva Stadium in Dublin – but I don't recall who it was against!"

EVAN FERGUSON

FACT FILE

POSITION: FORWARD
HEIGHT: 1.88M (6FT 2IN)
BIRTH DATE: 19 OCTOBER 2004
BIRTH PLACE: BETTYSTOWN, IRELAND

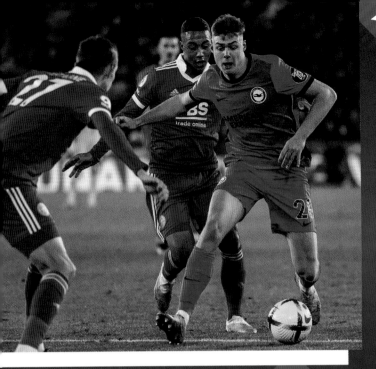

Q: Have you enjoyed working under Robert De Zerbi?

"He's been really good – obviously he and Graham Potter are two different characters. We've qualified for Europe, and it shows how quickly we've progressed."

Q: Manchester City manager Pep Guardiola has described Brighton as one of the best teams in world football – how does that feel?

"Coming from a man like that, it's obviously a big compliment for all of us. It shows the hard work we're putting in every day is bringing results and getting attention from a bigger audience."

Q: Who did you support as a kid?

Manchester United. It's kind of weird playing up front alongside Danny Welbeck because he was in the United team I used to support! We have a laugh and a joke about it, and it just shows how fast football can go."

Q: When did you think you had a real chance of making it as a professional footballer?

"I don't think there's just one moment when you think that – football goes so quickly and things can happen very fast and the next moment you're there, playing in the Premier League. When the chance does come, you feel you need to impress every time because of the competition for places."

Q: What made you choose Brighton?

"The feeling I got from the club when I first got here. They showed me the pathway and how you can actually make it coming through the academy, so that's the main reason."

Q: Do you enjoy living on the south coast?

"I lived by the sea in Ireland but it's a different sort of beach in Brighton – all stoney! I've settled in well and I'm enjoying it here, it's a nice place to live, especially in the summer and I enjoy going out trying different restaurants. There's plenty to choose from and I enjoy Thai the best."

Q: The 2022/23 season has been fantastic for you – has it been beyond your own expectations?

"In all honesty I didn't have any expectations to exceed! I didn't set any personal goals or targets, so it hasn't gone beyond anything because I've just taken it on a game-by-game basis. I wanted to get my first Premier League goal, of course, but as I say, I didn't want to look too far ahead because everything in football changes so quickly."

Q: What's it like playing in this Brighton team?

"It just feels right. Everyone knows what to do and how to do it. Everyone has each other's back."

Q: What's your advice for any youngsters wanting to follow in your footsteps?

"Just listen to your coaches along the way, work hard and you'll get there one day."

VAR

Love it or hate it, **VAR** is here to stay. Do you think it has made football better or worse? Does anyone even understand how the **VAR** process works? Whether you do or not, here is the complete Shoot guide to VAR...

WHAT DOES VAR STAND FOR?

VAR stands for **V**ideo **A**ssistant **R**eferee

WHEN DID VAR FIRST BEGIN IN ENGLISH FOOTBALL?

VAR started for the first time during the 2019/20 Premier League season – this was after every Premier League side voted to have the technology introduced the season before.

DOES EVERY PREMIER LEAGUE GAME HAVE VAR?

Yes – all 380 games have a VAR monitoring the game – plus an Assistant VAR!

WHAT DOES THE VAR LOOK FOR?

The VAR is there to spot 'clear and obvious' or 'serious missed incidents', meaning major moments that the on-field referee has missed or not aware of. Offsides, goals, penalties and sending off decisions are all scrutinised by the VAR, and it even checks for mistaken identity!

EXPLAINED

WHEN VAR SUGGESTS THE ON-FIELD REFEREE CHECKS THE PITCH-SIDE MONITOR, DOES THEY HAVE TO CHANGE THEIR DECISION?

No - VAR recommends the referee watches the incident with the benefit of various TV angles. Ultimately, they then make their own decision, but a high percentage of these incidents ends with a reversal of the original decision.

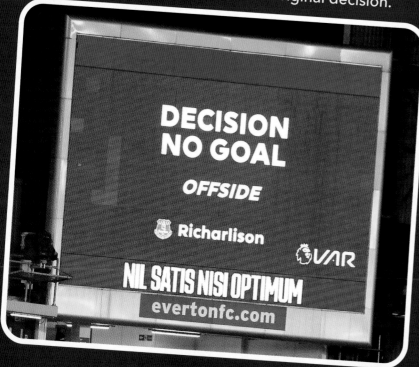

DECISION NO GOAL

OFFSIDE

Richarlison

VAR

NIL SATIS NISI OPTIMUM

evertonfc.com

DOES VAR GET IT RIGHT EVERY TIME?

No - the VAR makes a decision based on their understanding of the incident, but some decisions create plenty of debate! In short, the VAR is there to help as much as possible, but it will never achieve 100% accuracy.

DOES THE VAR DECISION HAVE A TIME LIMIT?

No - though the VAR will work as efficiently as possible to ensure the game continues without a major stoppage, on certain decisions, accuracy is more important than speed, so the VAR – in effect – can take as long as they want!

HOW DOES THE ON-FIELD REFEREE KNOW SOMETHING IS BEING REVIEWED?

If there is a passage of play or moment that needs to be looked at more closely, the VAR team will scrutinise the TV footage and then inform the referee via their earpiece. When that happens, the referee will inform the players that a review is in process.

DO YOU LIKE VAR?

WOULD YOU GIVE VAR A  OR ?

PEP'S UNSTOPPABLE MACHINE!

Pep Guardiola's Manchester City just keep rolling on! City made it three Premier League titles in a row after successfully chasing down Arsenal and then won the FA Cup against Manchester United and completed the famous treble by getting their hands on the Champions League trophy. Shoot takes a look at City's incredible stats under Pep's management – plus how the Blues got on in 2022/23!

TROPHIES

Premier League x 5
FA Cup x 2
League Cup x 4
Community Shield x 2
Champions League x 1

CITY'S RECORD UNDER PEP

Matches: 414
Wins: 301
Draws: 55
Defeats: 58
Goals: 1017
Conceded: 337

2022 / 23 LEAGUE POSITION

Position: 1st
Points: 89
Goals scored: 94
Goals against: 33

MEMORABLE MATCHES

CITY 6-3 Manchester United
Premier League
02/10/2022 - Etihad

City blew neighbours United out of the water, going in 4-0 up at half-time with two goals each for Erling Haaland and Phil Foden. Antony pulled one back after the break, but Haaland and Foden both completed their hat-tricks before Anthony Martial pulled back two late consolation goals.

CITY 4-0 Real Madrid
(City win 5-1 on aggregate)
Champions League semi-final second-leg
17/5/2022 - Etihad

City's painful Champions League semi-final loss the season before was avenged at the Etihad where City thrashed the reigning champions 4-0. After drawing 1-1 in the first leg, Bernardo Silva scored two first-half goals to put City in command and further goals from Manuel Akanji and Julian Alvarez sealed an emphatic win.

Arsenal 1-3 CITY
Premier League
15/02/2023 - The Emirates

Billed as the game that would decide the title, City had to win and when Kevin De Bruyne scored a superb goal on 24 minutes, it seemed as though that's what would happen. But Bukayo Saka's penalty levelled up matters and the game was back in the balance. But late goals from Jack Grealish and Erling Haaland sealed a wonderful 3-1 win to put City top of the league.

HOW WELL WILL CITY DO IN 2023 / 24?

FILL IN WHAT YOU THINK WILL HAPPEN!

Premier League final position:	
Points total:	
PL Goals scored:	
PL Goals against:	
Top goal scorer:	
Most assists:	
FA Cup:	
League Cup:	
Champions League:	
Club World Cup:	
European Super Cup:	

SUPER STATS

City went 25 matches unbeaten from the start of February to the end of May.

City completed a league double over nearest title challengers Arsenal, winning 3-1 at the Emirates and 4-1 at the Etihad.

Erling Haaland top scored on 52 goals for the season.

City took 52 out of a possible 57 points at the Etihad, scoring 60 goals - that's an average of more than three goals every home match!

Kevin De Bruyne's 16 Premier League assists was the best in the Premier League.

FINAL WINS

CHAMPIONS LEAGUE FINAL - 10/06/2023
CITY 1-0 Inter Milan
Atatürk Olympic Stadium, Istanbul

City won their first ever Champions League with a narrow victory over Italian side Inter Milan. The Blues had reached the final in 2021, but lost 1-0 to Chelsea and had also been in three Champions League semi-finals, so there was a feeling that Pep Guardiola would guide his players to become European champions sooner or later. The only goal of the game came when Spanish midfielder Rodrigo placed a powerful low drive past an unsighted keeper on 68 minutes. Inter had a couple of late chances to equalise, but City fully deserved the victory.

FA CUP FINAL - 03/06/2023
CITY 2-1 Manchester United
Wembley Stadium, London

The first ever FA Cup final to feature both Manchester teams did not disappoint. City took the lead after just 13 seconds when Ilkay Gundogan volleyed home from 20 yards to score the fastest FA Cup final goal ever! United were handed a lifeline (literally), when VAR decided Jack Grealish had handled the ball in the box for a United penalty that Bruno Fernandes scored. But City scored a second with another Gundogan volley on 51 minutes to win the game 2-1 and complete the coveted domestic 'double'.

STANDOUT STARS

JULIAN ALVAREZ
Position: Forward, Country: Argentina

Alvarez had a wonderful year for club and country. First he played a major role in Argentina's World Cup win in Qatar, scoring four goals and playing in the final. And in his first year as a Manchester City player, he scored 17 goals in 49 matches — many of those appearances from the bench — as well as winning Premier League and FA Cup winner's medals. Not a bad first season!

PHIL FODEN
Position: Midfielder, Country: England

The City and England playmaker is only 23-years-old, yet he has already made 217 appearances and had scored 60 goals going into the 2023/24 season. In that time, the Stockport Iniesta — as City fans nicknamed him — has won FIVE Premier League titles, TWO FA Cups, FOUR Carabao Cups, TWO FA Community Shield victories...oh, and one Champions League title! That's 14 major titles already — incredible!

BIZARRE FACTS

Brentford were the only team to complete a Premier League double over the champions.

Bottom of the league Southampton knocked City out of the Carabao Cup!

MY 2024

It's time to look into your crystal ball and predict the future! At the end of the 2023/24 season, you can check on how many predictions you got right.

ENGLISH LEAGUES CHAMPIONS 2023/24

PREMIER LEAGUE CHAMPIONS

....

CHAMPIONSHIP CHAMPIONS

....

LEAGUE ONE CHAMPIONS

....

LEAGUE TWO CHAMPIONS

....

PREMIER LEAGUE AWARDS

PLAYER OF THE SEASON

....

YOUNG PLAYER OF THE SEASON

....

MANAGER OF THE SEASON

....

GOLDEN BOOT

....

CHAMPIONS LEAGUE 2024

CHAMPIONS (MEN'S)

....

RUNNERS-UP

....

GOLDEN BOOT

....

CHAMPIONS (WOMEN'S)

....

RUNNERS-UP

....

CUP COMPETITIONS 2024

FA CUP WINNERS

....

EFL CUP WINNERS

....

WOMEN'S FA CUP WINNERS

....

WOMEN'S LEAGUE CUP WINNERS

....

PREDICTIONS +

WOMEN'S SUPER LEAGUE 2023/24

CHAMPIONS

....

RUNNERS-UP

....

GOLDEN BOOT

....

PLAYER OF THE SEASON

....

YOUNG PLAYER OF THE SEASON

....

SCOTTISH PREMIERSHIP 2023/24

CHAMPIONS

....

RUNNERS-UP

....

GOLDEN BOOT

....

PLAYER OF THE SEASON

....

YOUNG PLAYER OF THE SEASON

....

EUROPEAN LEAGUES CHAMPIONS

LA LIGA (SPAIN)

....

BUNDESLIGA (GERMANY)

....

LIGUE 1 (FRANCE)

....

SERIE A (ITALY)

....

IS FOOTBALL COMING HOME?

Can the Three Lions go one better than runners-up at Euro 2020 and finally bring football home as European Champions?

EURO 2024

CHAMPIONS

....

RUNNERS-UP

....

PLAYER OF THE TOURNAMENT

....

SHOOT'S WOMEN'S ULTIMATE WORLD XI

Women's football has never been more popular, especially after the 2023 FIFA Women's World Cup.

With record crowds attending matches all over the world to watch the best players around, what better time to bring you Shoot's Ultimate Women's World XI.

Below are the players who we feel deserve to be chosen – but we've left a space beneath each player for you to put your favourite stars in, just in case you don't agree with our selections.

GK — Mary EARPS

The Manchester United keeper has grown in stature over the past couple of years, making the Lionesses' No.1 jersey her own. Earps holds the record for most clean sheets in the WSL and is very much a safe pair of hands.

YOUR CHOICE ....

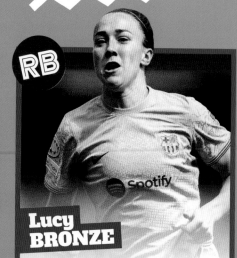

RB — Lucy BRONZE

The dynamic right-back has enjoyed a magnificent career so far at club level and with the Lionesses, where she is quite rightly regarded as a legend. She has played for many of Europe's top clubs and is currently with Barcelona.

YOUR CHOICE ....

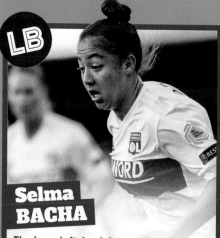

LB — Selma BACHA

The Lyon left-back has emerged as one of the best in Europe and aged just 22 will only get better and better. A multiple Champions League winner, she is fast and able to get many crosses into the box and assisting plenty of goals.

YOUR CHOICE ....

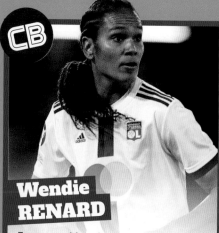

CB — Wendie RENARD

France and Lyon's experienced central defender is regarded as one of the best in the world. Fast, with excellent technique and a reputation for scoring thumping headers, Renard is closing in on 150 goals at club level!

YOUR CHOICE ....

CB
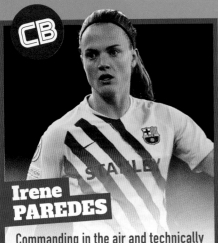

Irene PAREDES

Commanding in the air and technically gifted with the ball at her feet, Irene Paredes is a modern defender in every sense of the word. The Barcelona and Spain star also chips in with the odd goal here and there.

YOUR CHOICE ....

MF

Lauren HEMP

As one the Lionesses' most exciting talents, Hemp is destined for great things. An excellent and versatile left midfielder who can score spectacular goals. Aged just 23, she will become an even bigger talent in the years to come.

YOUR CHOICE ....

MF

Alexia PUTELLAS

Quite simply a magnificent footballer, Alexia Putellas has to be in our World XI. Often described as 'the perfect No.10', the Barcelona and Spain skipper would provide creativity, assists and goals for this team.

YOUR CHOICE ....

MF

Beth MEAD

The star of the Lionesses' Euro 2022 glory, Beth Mead has consistently shone for Arsenal and England over the past few seasons. Though injury kept her sidelined for much of 2022/23, the dashing winger's star continues to rise.

YOUR CHOICE ....

FW

Sam KERR

A prolific goal-scorer who is one of the game's top strikers. The Chelsea and Australia forward can score all types of goals and is a threat anywhere. She has scored almost 300 goals for club and country – a phenomenal record.

YOUR CHOICE ....

FW

Vivianne MIEDEMA

The WSL record goal-scorer has close to a goal-a-game record for Arsenal, Netherlands and throughout her career. A truly gifted forward who can use both feet and has a classy style of play that makes her one of the best.

YOUR CHOICE ....

FW

Bunny SHAW

The Caribbean goal machine – Khadija 'Bunny' Shaw has scored 48 goals in 55 matches for Manchester City in her first two seasons as well as 55 goals in 38 matches for Jamaica! A natural goal-scorer who has her best years in front of her.

YOUR CHOICE

....

Do you agree? Is your favourite player included? Add your selections to the boxes below each player if you think they deserve to be part of the team.

ANSWERS

10 PENALTY SHOOTOUT

1. 2 goals
2. 7-0
3. 4 managers
4. 4 managers
5. 9 seconds
SD. 90,000

11 FROM THE SPOT

A. MISS
B. Bottom Left
C. Bottom Left

12-13
HAIR-Y STYLES

A: Reece James & Mykhailo Mudryk
B: Bruno Fernandes & Antony
C: Erling Haaland & Jack Grealish
D: Aaron Ramsdale & Ben White
E: Miguel Almirón & Bruno Guimarães
F: Virgin van Dijk & Trent Alexander-Arnold

CELEBRATIONS

A: Son Heung-min
B: Ellen White
C: Marcus Rashford
D: Mo Salah
E: Erling Haaland
F: Harry Kane

WHAT'S MY NUMBER?

Sterling - 17
Dunk - 5
Eze - 10
Foden - 47
Robertson - 26
Isak - 14

15 CAREER CHANGE

1. Andy Robertson
2. Jude Bellingham
3. Danny Welbeck
4. Raheem Sterling

16 HIT OR MISS?

GAME 1: Hit   GAME 2: Miss
GAME 3: MIss   GAME 4: Hit

22-23 WORLD CLUB WORDSEARCH

ENGLAND: Liverpool, Arsenal, Manchester United
FRANCE: Monaco
PORTUGAL: Porto, Benfica
ARGENTINA: River Plate
SCOTLAND: Celtic
GERMANY: Bayern Munich, Wolfsburg, Red Bull Leipzig
UKRAINE: Dynamo Kyiv
NETHERLANDS: Ajax
SPAIN: Real Madrid, Barcelona, Real Sociedad
ITALY: Juventus, Inter Milan
BELGIUM: Anderlecht
GREECE: Olympiacos

24-25 STADIUM MYSTERY

1. Tottenham Hotspur, Tottenham Hotspur Stadium
2. Liverpool, Anfield
3. Manchester City, Etihad Stadium
4. Fulham, Craven Cottage
5. Arsenal, The Emirates
6. Newcastle United, St James Park

26-27 SHOOT'S SUPER QUIZ - 1ST HALF

1. Manchester City
2. Aston Villa
3. Luton Town
4. False, Barcalona have 5, Bayern Munich have 6
5. Crystal Palace
6. Video
7. Brighton & Hove Albion
8. Wrexham
9. Sarina Wiegman
10. The Blades
11. Bruno Fernandes
12. True
13. Manchester United
14. Newcastle United
15. West Ham United
16. Manchester City
17. Roy Hodgson
18. Scotland
19. Plymouth Argyle
20. False, he plays for Portugal

30 GUESS WHO?

PLAYER 1: Jack Grealish
PLAYER 2: Bukayo Saka
PLAYER 3: Mo Salah
PLAYER 4: Callum Wilson

36-37 SPOT THE BALL

GAME 1: Ball E
GAME 2: Ball B
GAME 3: Ball E
GAME 4: Ball B

52-52 THE ULTIMATE CHAMPIONS LEAGUE QUIZ

1. Real Madrid (14 wins)
2. Benfica
3. Manchester City
4. True
5. Ronaldo
6. Ronaldo
7. 16 goals
8. True
9. 15 goals
10. 4 red cards
11. Erling Haaland
12. The European Cup
13. Leeds United
14. True – between 1977-82
15. False, only Celtic
16. Milan
17. 4 times
18. 3 times
19. Rodri
20. Wolfsburg

54 SPOT THE DIFFERENCE

58-59 SHOOT'S SUPER QUIZ - 2ND HALF

21. Real Madrid
22. Wolverhampton Wanderers
23. False
24. Hammerhead
25. Leicester City
26. 12 yards
27. Blackburn Rovers
28. Marc Guéhi
29. Everton
30. Fishing
31. True
32. One
33. Ajax
34. Son Heung-min

35. Napoli
36. Chelsea
37. False
38. 3 goals (not including the penalty shootout)
39. Chloe Kelly
40. True

62 TRANSFER CHALLENGE

César Azpilicueta: £7m
Andrew Robertson: £8m
Seamus Coleman: £60k
Alexis Mac Allister: £7m
Michail Antonio: £7m

(Information/figures correct as of: July 2023)